know
the
game

English f[olk dancin]g

By Jack Hamilton

GW00394362

Produced in collaboration with

the ENGLISH FOLK DANCE AND SONG SOCIETY

EP Publishing Ltd.

CONTENTS

Introduction

By tradition, Friday and Saturday nights are nights out for dancing, but the 'Threepenny Hop' is no longer with us. Instead, at mainly private functions up and down the country, there are thousands of 'Barn Dances'. Some are called 'Square Dances', 'Country Dances', 'Hoe-downs' or 'Western Nights' but the most common name used today is Barn Dance. Each consists of a programme of sociable dances in group formations in the idiom of contemporary English Folk Dance. This book aims to introduce you to this enjoyable activity painlessly and help you to take the floor with ease. A book is no substitute for the real thing: one dance is worth a thousand words about it.

There are two main kinds of English 'folk' dance: the ritual dances, performances by men only such as the Morris dance, and the social dances for men and women to be enjoyed as any other form of ballroom dancing. Some readers may have seen folk dancing by young school children and from this gained an impression of a childish activity. Not so. The material is usually adapted to childish needs and the dance assumes a quite different purpose when adults are involved.

This book is about contemporary English folk dancing for men and women.

As a common denominator for folk of all ages, it appeals equally to those with and without ballroom skills. All the dances are group dances and, in the hands of a competent 'Caller' with a sensitive band, there is no limit to the enjoyment of any individual in the room. People taking part for the first time are always astonished at how much they achieve so easily: this is attributable to the 'folk' element in the dances and music as well as to the skill of the caller. Because of its wide appeal— some other forms of dance have become so specialised that they rely upon great expertise or a competitive element for their enjoyment, or appeal to only one age group—organisers of sociable events are finding the perfect answer to their problems in the contemporary English folk dance, the Barn Dance.

Most countries have some form of social group dance in their folk lore. Some have chosen to fossilise the material into a display of dance of a bygone era while others have refashioned their dance heritage into spectacular display sometimes exhibiting great gymnastic skill or producing a balletic stage show. This is fundamentally different from the commonly accepted meaning of 'folk' in England when referring to social dance. English folk dances are for participation. But, confusingly, social dances are sometimes dressed up for a particular occasion: this is the exception. Normal dress for a barn dance is what you like wearing—unless the organiser has indicated a theme of dress for the evening.

We refer to our dances as being of a 'living' tradition. This means that they are allowed to evolve in common usage over the centuries. While most of the dances in this book cannot be traced back much more than one century, their antecedents are very much older. However ingenious the caller may be at inventing a new figure, it is unlikely that the figure and the sequence of figures for a 'new' dance were not invented long ago but fell out of fashion perhaps, or simply never stood the test of time. However, such dances are of the essence of the 'living' tradition because they are almost always a re-hash of older dance figures put to a new or different tune. Even for an old dance, the old associated tune is not necessarily used exclusively: part of the fun is in adapting to the latest fashion in tunes. The tradition happily absorbs such influences and thereby ensures its ever contemporary appeal.

The Room

The shape of the 'sets', groups of dancers, varies with each dance. The illustrations on page 5 represent some common situations. The man always has his partner on his right except when facing her in a long set. The 'calls'

Top and
1st couple

2nd

up

3rd

down

4th

LONG SET
(partners facing)

Top of room

Band – Caller

facing centre

1st couple

2nd

4th

3rd

SQUARE SET

are always to the man and may refer to a particular couple or dancer—'first couple', 'third lady' or 'side couples'—sometimes only one dancer is moving at a time and sometimes the whole set.

Dance Figures

Many of the dances you will meet at an evening of Barn Dance are a mixture of a few basic two-handed (two people) and four-handed (four people) patterns of movement which we call figures. Infinite variety is obtained from using different shapes of set (group) and rhythm and tunes as well as progression by couples moving on to dance with another couple and even changing partner. Here are some of the common figures you will meet:

STAR sometimes called 'Right Hands Across' for two couples facing—the two men take right hands, the two girls take right hands below the men's (an ordinary hand-shaking hold is usual) and rotate the star by moving forwards (Fig. 1) .At the halfway point of the phrase of music, change hands to left and reverse the direction of the star . . . to places.

Fig. 1

HANDS FOUR is the callers way of saying join hands in a ring of four facing inwards, and circle around to the left (Fig 2). At the halfway point of the music, circle back to the right . . . to places.

Fig. 2

Once you start moving with the music, you will sense this 'halfway point'. You could count eight steps but that would be arithmetic: and this happens to be a dancing session. You can be sure that the music itself, and probably the caller too, will tell you when to reverse.

And when you take a girl's hand in a circle formation it is conventional for the man's palm to be uppermost to receive the girl's hand (Fig. 3).

Fig. 3

LADIES CHAIN is one of the most pleasurable movements in the game. For two couples facing:

Man hands his partner forward towards the other girl (Fig. 4). The girls take right hands and pass around each other towards the other man.

Fig. 4

Fig. 5

The other man takes the new girl's left hand in his left, places his right hand behind her waist (and into her right hand placed ready, palm outermost, just above the right buttock) and pivots her forward with a gentle push (Fig. 5) around into the place which his partner has just vacated. The girl meanwhile leans ever so gently on his right arm in appreciation.

The whole movement is then repeated to places—and all this pleasure has occupied only eight bars of music.

RIGHT AND LEFT THROUGH. For two couples facing—or, depending on the formation of the particular dance, could be side by side—the track of the movements is the same.

Fig. 6

Fig. 7

Move forward, crossing the set, and pass the opposite dancer by the right shoulder (Fig. 6). Turn to face the dancer now beside you. Give left hands and pass each other's left shoulder (Fig. 7). Face across the set again and repeat the two parts of that movement to places.

This figure is sometimes danced without giving hands: and sometimes with hands all the way.

Fig. 8   *Fig. 9*

PROMENADE occurs in every other dance. Side by side with partner, take her right hand in yours, then her left hand in yours below the right. This way the man has control over the girl's direction of movement and can guide her anywhere (Fig. 8).

Equally common, and a personal choice as appropriate, the man may take the girl's left hand in his and place his right hand around her waist as in the LADIES CHAIN hold (Fig. 9).

GRAND CHAIN can be danced whenever the set of dancers is facing inwards. Partners face each other and give right hands (Fig. 10). Move forward, passing partner to meet next girl with left hand (Fig. 11). Pass her and give right to the next . . . and so on following the call or until meeting your own partner again.

Fig. 10

Fig. 11

Fig. 12

Fig. 13

DO-SI-DO is a figure for two dancers, not necessarily partners. Face each other, walk forward passing right shoulders (Fig. 12), step to the right, retire (Fig. 13) to place passing left shoulders.

This is sometimes followed by a Do-si-do by the left, that is starting by passing left shoulders.

LEAD. Most dances require a 'leading' couple. It is the couple who is leading the dance at that moment, sometimes called the 'active' couple. The call may require a couple to 'lead' to the right, or to another couple . . . the man takes charge and leads his partner as required. At the end of a dance he may lead her to a chair.

BALANCE is a courtesy movement, preceding another. It is an individual movement and may in theory take any form you care to invent. In common practice it is usually a simple transfer of weight first onto the right foot, then onto the left. It is a stationary 'waltz' step. 'Balance' your weight onto the right foot, let the left follow to take the weight momentarily, then 'balance' onto the left foot, right following. Nearly always there is time to repeat this movement. Arms, with no partner to hold on to, should complement the balancing in any way that comes naturally. The balance is a preparation for the movement which follows.

and **SWING**—you will certainly do a lot of this. Balance and Swing frequently go together. There are several variations of hold but only two steps. The hold is a personal thing and the step depends broadly upon whether the dance is of American or English origin. The common American step is a walk-swing: in England, the pivot-swing. The principle of each is the same.

Ballroom Hold

The man takes control of his partner by placing his right hand firmly under the girl's left shoulder blade and his left hand clasps her right at a comfortable semi-extended shoulder height. The girl's left arm lies along the man's right with her hand on his right shoulder (Fig. 14).

Fig. 14

Walk Swing

With ballroom hold, dancers 'walk' around each other about a point between the outside of each right foot (Fig. 15/16) while exerting a comfortable centrifugal force by leaning slightly away from each other.

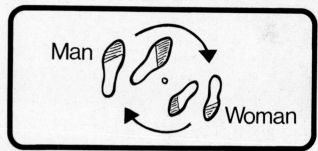

Fig. 15

Fig. 16

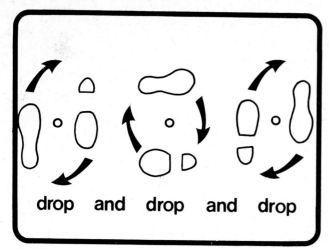

Fig. 17

Fig. 18

Pivot Swing

Hold and foot positions are as for Walk Swing but the step is more vigorous and exciting. The right foot is used differently from the left. The right is the 'pivot' and the left is the 'scooter'. Anticipate the beat, pushing with the left foot to drop (on the beat) onto the right (Fig. 17, 18). Pivot. The left foot momentarily takes the weight while the right foot pivots to the next drop.

Notation

English folk dance tunes are almost always in binary form, that is, in two parts, A and B. Each part is repeated to give a pattern AABB. Each A and each B is eight bars of music and each bar of music has two strong beats to which the dancer steps. So there are sixteen steps to each A or B music.

There are some exceptions. In a waltz, for example, there is only one main beat to each bar indicating only one main step.

In writing out instructions for dances (the dance notation), the tune and the dance are related by referring to A1 (first time) or A2 (the repeat) and B1 and B2.

Some dances are longer and require a third B music, B3. Some have a total length requiring the AABB to be played more than once. In this case the notation will indicate A3, A4, B3, B4 and so on.

While it is convenient to divide dances into 8-bar figures, in practice each figure should flow into the next without pause. When the sequence has been grasped and the book put down, the influence of good dancing music should make this apparent.

When dancers are in a 'set' with a prescribed number of couples, the dance ends when each couple has had a 'turn'. In a progressive dance, with an unlimited number of couples, the dance ends when the caller considers that a pause is desirable: in practice this is usually between 3 and 6 minutes.

Dances

PINS AND NEEDLES

Music: Any jig.

Form: Progressive Long set. Men side by side facing partners.

A1   Balance four in line. 1st couples give right hands and turn half round to stand between 2nd couples (Fig. 19) to whom they give left hands to form a line of four across the room (Fig. 20)—men are now facing down, girls facing up. This movement occupies four walkingsteps only. Four in line balance right and left.

Fig. 19

Top

Bottom of Set

Fig. 20

Top

Bottom of Set

Fig. 21

1st couples keep left hands, turn corner partner half round into line facing other direction and balance again (Fig. 21).

A2   Continue the movement: turn half with the left again and balance R and L. 1st couples only turn half with the right hand and balance to each other.

B1   1st couples lead down the set, turn, lead back to 2nd couple's place: 2nd couple having moved up in to 1st couple's place (progression).

(Fig. 24, page 19.)

B2   1st and 2nd couples dance once around each other into new places for the next turn of the dance (with another couple). Use a balance, or pas-de-bas step, with ballroom hold.

17

NOTTINGHAM SWING

Music: Any Hornpipe such as 'Paddy McGinty's Goat'.

Form: Progressive Long Set.

A   1st man and 2nd girl link right arms and swing (Fig. 22) with a 'step-hop' (step onto R with strong beat of music, then 'hop'—very small one—on the 'off' beat; step onto L etc.). 2nd man with 1st girl the

Fig. 22

I
&
2

and back

Fig. 23

18

Fig. 24

same. Take half the phrase of music each. Each couple takes four bars (8 steps).

B   1st couple join hands, dance two side steps down (Fig. 23) the set and two back. Separate, cast outside the set (Fig. 24) to 2nd couple's place while 2nd couple move up into first couple's place.

All swing partners in position with the same stephop. (Continue with the next couple down the set, repeating the sequence. On reaching either end of the set, remain alone for one sequence then rejoin the set with a different couple number.)

TIMBER SALVAGE REEL

Music: Any reel.

Form: Progressive long set. 1st couples change places. 1s face down, 2s face up (Fig. 25.)

A1 Do-si-do with the one below (Fig. 26). Do-si-do with partner.

A2 1st couples balance and swing.

B1 1st couples lead down the middle, back, cast outside around 2nd couple (progression).

B2 Right hand star. Left hand back.

etc

Fig. 25

Fig. 26

BLAYDON RACES

Music: 'The Blaydon Races' or anything similar.

Form: Circle, facing inwards.

A1   All to the centre and back. Repeat.

A2   Take partner in Ballroom hold. Chassé two steps to centre (Fig. 27) and back. Repeat.

B1   Promenade partner (Fig. 28)

B2   Men move forward to next girl in front. Balance and swing her, (put new partner on R, join hands in circle ready for A1).

Fig. 27

Fig. 28

WALTZ COUNTRY DANCE

Music: Any 32-bar waltz plus 8-bar 'waltz-on'. Or 40-bar waltz.

Form: Sicilian Circle—couple facing couple around the room (Fig. 29).

A1 Face opposite, give right hand. Balance forward and back (Fig. 30), forward again and change places. Face partner (Fig. 31), repeat.

A2 As above.

etc

Fig.
22

etc

Fig. 30

Fig. 31

B1 Join hands in a ring. Balance forward and back; pass left hand girl across (Fig. 32) to right hand girl's place (girls turning right as they cross). Repeat.

B2 As above.

B3 Waltz partner past this couple and on to the next one facing.

Fig. 32

CIRCASSIAN CIRCLE

Music: Any reel or jig.

Form: Hands joined in one circle facing in. Girl on man's right...

A1 Forward and back twice.
A2 Girls to centre and back.

Men to centre and back to left hand girl (Fig. 33).
B1 Swing new partner.
B2 Promenade new partner (Fig. 34) around the ring.

Fig. 33

Fig. 34

CUMBERLAND SQUARE EIGHT

Music: 'My Love She's but a Lassie yet' or any reel or
       jig.

Form: Square set of four couples.

A1   Top couples (either diagonal pair) Galop across
       (Fig. 35) set (passing) and back.
A2   Side couples the same.

B1   Top couples right hands across, left hands back.
B2   Sides the same.
A3   Top couples 'basket' to the left (Fig. 36).
A4   Sides the same.
B3   Join hands in a ring: Circle left.
B4   All promenade partner to place.

Fig. 35

Fig. 36

THE CUMBERLAND REEL

Music: Any reel or jig.

Form: Long set for four, five or six couples.

A1 Top two couples right hands across and back with left.

A2 1st couple down the centre and back.

B1 1st couple separate, cast outside the set to the bottom—other dancers follow—make an arch with partner for other dancers to promenade under (Fig. 37) to reform the set.

B2 All promenade to the left (Fig. 38), round into new places. (original 1st couple is now at the bottom). New top couple now leads.

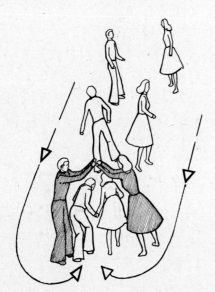

Fig. 37

Fig. 38

YORKSHIRE SQUARE EIGHT

Music: Any lively reel with polka rhythm.

Form: Four couples in a 'square', one couple on each side.

A1 Head couples (1st and 3rd) advance, retire, polka across.

A2 Side couples the same.

B1 Head couples the same to places.

B2 Side couples the same.
Head couples face to their right—

A3 1st and 2nd couples right hands across (Fig. 39) and back while 3rd and 4th the same.

A4 Same couples Ladies Chain.
Head couples face to their left—

B3 1st and 4th couples right hands across and back while 2nd and 3rd do the same.

B4 Same couples Ladies Chain.

A5 Girls to the centre and back. While they come back, men go to the centre, turn (Fig. 40) to swing the girl on the left.

A6 Promenade new partner to man's place

B5 and 6 as A5 and 6.

A7 and 8 as A5 and 6.

B7 and 8 as A5 and 6 to finish in original places with original partner.

Fig. 39

Fig. 40

LA RUSSE

Music: 'La Russe' or any similar reel.

Form: Square set as for 'Yorkshire Square'.

Introduction: first four bars of the tune to honour partner and corner girl.

A1　Man moves behind partner to right hand girl (who moves to meet him) (Fig.41). All balance and swing.

Fig. 42

A2　Return to places. All balance and swing partners.

B1　1st couple (leading couple) swing.

B2　1st couple promenade inside the set to places.

A3　Leading and opposite couples cross the set (leading couple inside) (Fig. 42). Both change places with partner. Crossback (opposite couple inside). Change places with partner.

A4　As A3.

B3　All join hands, circle left.

B4　Promenade partners to places.
　　Whole sequence is then repeated with each other couple leading in turn; 2nd, 3rd, 4th.

Fig. 41

28

The Body

The dances have evolved over many centuries among communities of different climates and ways of life. These have tended to fuse together over the past few years especially under the influence of modern mass media. While there are still places and regions where particular styles, steps and repertoire continue as of tradition, most urban folk identify with an easy lilting step for many of the dances. So the step for some dances will be decided by local custom—in the Northern Counties, for example, where there has been a continuous and strong tradition of what we *now* call 'folk' dancing, most dancers would use a rant step throughout a dance. The rant, a variation of a polka step, has a strong ta-rum-tum-tum rhythm, closely following the accented beats of the rant tune. In the south, where there has been little continuous tradition of dance, the 'dance walk' is common.

Steps are indicated by the music which is divided between four rhythms: reel, jig, waltz and hornpipe. A reel is a march type of tune which has two steps to each bar of music. A jig is a similar pace but each beat of the two steps is divided into three parts um-pe-ty um-pe-ty. The waltz is different from that of the modern ballroom. It is a balance movement of the body right to left, the feet following the body. When you sway to the right the left foot follows with a feint step, taking weight for sufficiently long to allow the body to rotate, rhythmically followed by the right foot similarly and leaving the left foot free to follow the body in a sway to the left on the first beat of the next bar. So you have a pattern RIGHT left right, LEFT right left, but the feeling is of one strong beat (step) to each bar rather than three which would be felt with a slower ballroom waltz. The hornpipe is less common and no example is included in this book. The body movement is slower and the 'Pugwash' tune is a good example.

Right	and	left	and
one	and	two	and
step	and	step	and

the 'and' is a left of the other foot (sometimes a hop) and there are two steps to each bar as in a reel.

All the steps require a lilt, a giving to the music to a degree suggested by the atmosphere, your partner *and* the music.

In general, the music sometimes appears to emphasise the off-beat, the beat between the naturally strong accents, the pulse between the steps; this is characteristic of folk dance music and should induce a lift of the body so that movement is easy and 'dancey'. Ideally you should share this feeling of lift not only with your partner but with the whole set. Once you have experienced this little bit of magic, pass the book on to a friend: you have arrived.

The Music

Ever since the medieval Carole in which simple movement was integral with song, our folk dances have related closely with songs: many dances take their names from the song. Many more, however, have lost their song connection and are danced to any lively reel or jig at a fastish walking pace.

Most of the tunes derive from the traditional country fiddlers, handed down over the centuries, and demand a special kind of playing. 'Lift' is the most important ingredient of music for dance: it is concerned more with the 'off' beat than the 'down' beat; it is this which gives the dancer the impetus to carry him from one pulse to the next. The musical instrument must be made to 'dance' where players are normally concerned to make their instrument 'sing'.

The Caller

The Master of Ceremonies is a familiar figure to the English ballroom, but in America a 'Caller' fulfils this function. The Caller will give a lot more prompting of dances and figures than was the duty of the M.C. So, since it is more appropriate, we have adopted the Caller to introduce the dances and to remind us of the figures as they occur. By this means we are not required to memorise a large number of dances but instead lean upon the Caller's skill in order to enjoy a very great variety of dance material during the course of an evening of dance.

When each village community had its own repertoire of dances there was rather less need for a lot of calling. Today, however, in a room full of much travelled folk, more than one version of a dance may be known: it is the caller's duty to establish which version he wishes to be used.

His duties also include those of the more familiar Master of Ceremonies. He ensures that everyone present is partnered or has opportunity to meet the other dancers in a 'mixer' dance. He controls the programme, the band, the length of dances and the pace of the evening as well as the order of events.

America

In the seventeenth century in rural England what we now call 'folk' dance was a normal activity; there was no other form of social dance—only a difference between the dances of the Court and those of the people. It was from this period that a great movement of people from village communities into towns began. With it came the decline of cottage crafts and social skills. Fortunately there was also a movement westwards across the Atlantic and these English skills were transplanted into a rural New England where they thrived on assuming a new importance such as they had once enjoyed in the homeland. These skills included dance.

We owe much to this historical situation because while in England dances were falling into disuse and were no longer handed down within village communities, the same dances became a social necessity again in newly settled communities in America. It could be said that the folk dance of England was nearly smothered by industrialisation but took on a new lease of life in America where life more closely followed the pattern of a previous century in England; certainly life proceeded more slowly by comparison.

So it is that many dances were taken to America, well used and moulded to the slightly different social climate, evolved with the years and now come back to us excitingly fresh but still recognisably English. There are many cases of 'English' dances being 'lost' to this country which have been recovered as good as new after perhaps a hundred years of usage abroad.

Today, most callers will include in their programme some native, some recovered and some American dances. Our tradition and enjoyment is thereby enriched.

Glossary of Common Terms

Balance	Usually precedes a swing, a preparatory or courtesy movement where weight is put on to right foot, then left. Variations are infinite, optional and individual.
Basket	In a circle formation, men take girls around waists and girls rest arms on men's shoulders. Pivot step, usually to the left.
Cast	To turn away from the set (usually to lead down the outside) by turning up and around.
Chassé	Stepping sideways.
Contra	Progressive longways.
Contrary partner	The other girl or man in a four handed set.
Corner	In a square set, the dancer nearest— on the man's left, the girl's right.
Dip and Dive	For two couples facing; couples pass alternately over and under arches formed by partners joining nearest hands.
Do-Si-Do	Face partner (or other dancer as directed) walk forward to pass right shoulders, move to right, retire to place passing left shoulders. There are many regional variations of this expression both in spelling and in execution.
Double step	Lift *R* L R, lift *L* R L, variously known as rant or polka step, and belongs with rant tunes.
Elbow Swing	Swing with right (or left) arms linked by the crook of the elbow.
Galop	Sidestepping movement, partners facing, in either direction. (N.B. quadrupeds gallop).
Half Promenade	Promenade to change places with couple facing.
Hands four	Four dancers join hands in a ring.
Honour	Bow or similar acknowledgment.
Improper	Man in girl's place.
Inside hands	Nearest hand to partner.
Lift	Rising movement having the feel of a skip but in which the foot barely leaves the floor.
Long Set	A set of men facing partners in which the top couple ends each sequence at the bottom to create a new top couple.
Opposite	Contrary.
Pivot step	Commonly used for the swing: also known as a 'buzz' step. See photograph. Ballroom hold, weight mainly on right foot placed (out)side by (out)side, pivoting by 'dropping' onto the right foot using the left to transfer the weight for each 'drop'.
Polka step	Rant step, double step.

Progressive	Any dance where couples progress to another couple after each sequence.
Promenade	Couples side by side, right hands joined over left hands. There are several variations of this hold.
Prompt Call	The caller's reminder of the next figure—given in time for its execution with the appropriate music.
Proper	Regular, normal formation. Usually relates to a longways set where man has partner on his right when facing 'up'.
Quadrille	Square set formed by four couples as 'La Russe'. One couple on each side of the square.
Rant step	Polka step, double step.
Reel	Tune in even time. A Dance. A weaving figure.
Right and Left Through	For two couples—a miniature grand chain. Cross the set passing partner R, turn to face dancer beside you, pass L. Repeat movements to places. There are many variations of this movement but in the most frequently used version it is usual to give left hands when passing, but not the right.
Right Hands Across	For two couples facing. Men join right hands, girls join hands under, rotate 'star' in clockwise direction.

	Change to left hands to return.
Right Hand Star	As Right Hands Across.
Set	Any dance formation.
Set Dance	A long set (as opposed to a circle or square) for a prescribed number of couples.
Sicilian Circle	Couple facing couple in a circle around the room.
Swing and Change	In a progressive dance; couples change places during a swing.
Threesome	Man or girl with two partners—one on either side.

Record

A stereo LP record containing all ten dances is available to accompany this book. Recorded by the Southerners band and entitled Know the Game, English Folk Dancing (Record No. KTG 12) it costs £2·00 plus 20p for postage and packing and is available from the Folk Shop, 2 Regents Park Road, London NW1 7AY. (Tel.: 01 485 2206). In case of any difficulty please contact Alan Corkett, 118 Little Bookham Street, Bookham, Surrey.

Printed by J. WARD & CO., Dewsbury

Play the Game

This fast-growing series now has the distinction of being partly international in origin as well as in readership. Four additions, written by top coaches in Germany and translated into English specially for the series, are: **TENNIS UP TO TOURNAMENT STANDARD, RIDING, SAILING** and **TABLE TENNIS**. These fully illustrated hardbacks at £1·75 have the clear aim of helping to take the beginner through from basics to competition grade.

Tennis sets out in simple form all the factors that go into making good strokes. It's strong on tactics and it also covers the crucial aspect of getting into peak physical shape.

Riding has its priorities right. It schools the rider to school the horse . . . for showjumping and dressage as well as country rideouts.

The ultra-modern *Sailing* carries over no anachronisms from the days when sailing was a pastime that only the wealthy could take up. It's a textbook on the proper handling, for relaxation or under racing conditions, of boat types that almost anyone can own nowadays.

Table Tennis makes a dual approach to the matter of upgrading performance. It's specially designed for use by both the learner on his own at home and the club leader coaching groups.

In-demand books in the series that are continually reappearing in new editions are *Cricket* (60p) *Coach Yourself Association Football* (£1) and a BHS *Riding* (60p).

ep sport

tennis–up to tournament standard

coach yourself association football

CRICKET
HOW TO PLAY
Produced for the P.C.C.

ep **THE EP GROUP OF COMPANIES**
EP Publishing Limited
Bradford Road, East Ardsley
Wakefield, Yorkshire WF3 2JN